Glimpses

from A longer view

BRENDA PEDDIGREW

November, 2022

Glimpses
Copyright © 2023 by Brenda Peddigrew

All rights reserved. No part of this publication may be reproduced, distributed, or transmitted in any form or by any means, including photocopying, recording, or other electronic or mechanical methods, without the prior written permission of the author, except in the case of brief quotations embodied in critical reviews and certain other non-commercial uses permitted by copyright law.

Cover photo by Brenda Peddigrew

Tellwell Talent
www.tellwell.ca

ISBN
978-1-77941-327-7 (Paperback)

This collection is dedicated to AyunaJoan: constant, steady, generous companion for the past twenty-five years — for her healing knowledge and loving patience, and for opening to me the natural world…as well as for her dog companions, one after another: Kassi, Kai, and now Mahti, ten years old as I write this.

Table of Contents

Joan: Tender Warrior 1
Complete 3
Ripening 4
Early Morning Minute 5
Blackbird Cabin 6
Trees 8
The Driver 9
A Sudden Shining 10
Just As You Are 12
The Silence 14
Home 15
Driven 16
Not Contradictions 18
Undoing 19
Loons 21
The Presence 22
Raggedy 23
Gaze and Wait 24
Waiting 26
The Heart's Senses 27
A Sense of Dying 28
Vibrations of Love 30
The Tenderness of Trees 31
Stop 32
Stopping 33
Life's Spiral: Giving Gold 34
Falling Away 36
The Line of Time 38
Mahti (Little Bear) 40
Stones of Invitation 41

A Bouquet of Grace	43
The River	45
Whirling Grace	46
A Smoothing	47
Tree	48
Claimed	49
Light	51
Unknowing	52
Stars	53
The Day Came	54
A Peak	55
The Fire	56
Suddenly	57
Opening	58
Taken	59
Spark	60
Whatever Life…	61
Beautiful Friend	63
Inner Flames	64
Still	69
Morning Stillness	70
Coasting Down the Hill	71
Doesn't Know	73
Alive! Alive!	74
Time Now…	77
Waters of Grace	79
Stirring of the World	81
Falling Apart	82
Tender Moments	84
Opening Arms	85
Forgetting/Remembering Everything	86
The Only Light	88
Dark Light	89
Chosen	90
Always Held	91
Steady Ground	92
All Light	93

Rhythm	95
I Don't Know	96
Return	98
Six Ducks	99
Stop and Wait	102
Burning	103
Breaking the Habit	104
Welcoming…	106
Revelation	107
Glance of Heaven	109
Making Way	110
Heart's Companion	112
Alive, Alive!	113
Portal	114
The Real Treasure	115
Presence	118
It's Enough	119
Emptying	121
In the Fullness	123
Home	124
Ashes	125
Spacing the Day	126
Poem of an Ordinary Day	128
Sitting in the Dark	129
For Robert*: Home	131
Release	133
Loving the Night	134
Presence	135
Doorway* (Thanksgiving Day 2020)	137
Lit By Stars/Holding Us All	139
Led By Light	141
Words	142
Resting in Light	144
The Sea Herself	145
No Words: Morning Comfort	146
Shimmering	148
Arriving	149

Rest	150
Finally	151
Womb of the World	152
Deep Surrender: Gutted	153
Only in Silence, Only in Light	155
Empty Fullness: Cosmos of the Heart	156
Home	157
The Great Emptiness*	158
Eggshells	160
Light Arrives	161
Silence:	162
Beside the Point	163
Fallen Away	164
All Else Falls Away	165

Out of the rubble of my dissolving life after the arrest of many priests in the Archdiocese of St. John's, NL, (where I had held the position of Director of Adult Faith Development)—arrests for sexually abusing boys in the hundreds—I struggled with shock the extent of which I had not experienced before. For this reason, I came to Toronto, lost and disoriented, seeking and finding healing help and space to breathe.

It did not help as I had hoped, and when I returned to St. John's after a year, I knew that my entire world had shifted, and was not in any way retrievable. I moved back to Ontario, this time to Huntsville, where Marge Denis, whom I had met the year before, had invited me to be one of the process facilitators who were hired by companies, religious orders, dioceses, and some government departments, to facilitate their meetings, including many Chapters of religious communities of men and women. And so I traveled to many parts of Canada, the U.S., Ireland, and ultimately Nicaragua (the Sisters of St. Agnes); then Zambia and Zimbabwe for the Presentation Sisters of Ireland whose missions were there, and for whom I had spent many months facilitating meetings for them in Ireland itself, including a month at Dromantine in the North.

But after five years of this work and living in Huntsville – which meant traveling to Toronto Airport, a two-hour drive and then back after every contract, I decided to move to Etobicoke, for one reason only: to be close to the Airport!

While in Huntsville I had worked with a naturopath regularly. So I asked her for a reference to a naturopath close to where I was moving in Etobicoke. Lo and behold: it was Dr. Joan Weir, N.D., at the Scott Health Clinic in Woodbridge!

I had not worked long with Joan, when she took a canoe trip to the far north with three men as fellow paddlers. Not only was this trip beyond difficult and painful for her in the company of these three men, but she had just lost her only sister. On Joan's return, and knowing of my own work as a counsellor and spiritual guide, she asked if she could talk to me professionally; thus we agreed to suspend our doctor/patient relationship so that I could hear Joan's grief and the effects of that fateful trip.

From then on, Joan and I were firm friends. She invited me on canoe trips to Temagami with her every August for several summers- God bless her patience. Eventually we decided to share a house on 77 Mill Road in Etobicoke, where I continued to travel and she saw patients as well. It was there I decided to pursue a doctoral degree with the California Institute of Integral Studies, and it was in the last year of earning that degree – that we decided it was best to leave Toronto altogether. So – a few days after my successful doctoral defense – we drove north and found quickly the house and property, which we called "SoulWinds" – and on which we still live after twenty-plus years.

And so it is to Joan that I dedicate the poems in this book. She opened doors and worlds to me, and supported my struggles and often hesitant and tentative adventures into the amazing forests and rivers and lakes among which we live and work and have our being. Without her, these poems might never have been given.

Brenda Peddigrew, 23 November, 2022

And here is my tribute poem to Joan:

Joan: Tender Warrior

The one who rescued me
from a sinking ship, when all the lines
holding my anchors – family, Church,
religious community – were cut, almost
all at once. The one who
rescues me still – every day,
every day, making it possible
to live in this nourishing forest,
daily blessed with tree silence,
river passing close, neighbours
friendly and helpful, all of us –
all of us – giving space to others,
and help when needed.

Joan is a tender warrior, without
whom I might not be living
at all, so traumatic were the years
of transformation, of everything
I knew and built my life around
all gone, transformed in the flash
of a magician's wand into
nothingness, into the opposite of
all it was before –

and then comes Joan: risker
adventurer, generous spirit,
healer and loving companion –
rebuilding my shattered soul, and
doing that still- today and every day.

*Joan is the strong woman of the woods,
compassionate healer, friend of
my heart, restorer of my soul,
and daily companion
of life and grace...
Joan is blessing and strength.
Together we create
an arc of love in our small, vibrant
and tender world, dogs and cats
included!*

Complete

This afternoon I spent time
With a tiny frog who was very still
On the wooden dock when I approached…
I also saw a Duck with 14 babies (14!)
swimming them away quickly at my approach.
I spent time with the frog,
whose stillness I envied…while
I watched the duck swim away,
all babies together.

When the frog tried to dive beneath
the dock in the space between
the boards, he got stuck, back legs
swinging in the air. I freed him
and set him under the dock, whole,
where his stillness inspires me.

My day is complete.

Ripening

A plum sits out
on the kitchen counter'
When I ask
why?
the answer is
"so it can ripen."

Ah! So ripening needs heat,
needs light, not the dark cold
of the fridge-

So does a person, really –
not dark cold,
but light and heat
pulsing into
life's fullness
of age and grace.

Early Morning Minute

I stand at the door
looking out the wet window. Rain
has poured down all night, and drips
are visible everywhere, even
from the needles of spruce and pine,
and the drooping stillness of all
the colorful flowers.

Change never stops. What I see
now will be gone by noon. The sun
will erase these shining drops, offering
light in shimmers and rainbow colors.
And isn't it the same
With us all? Here one minute
And gone the next? Isn't it?

But oh – that minute!
Full of glow and glory, giving
itself to a world waiting
for just the colors, just those –
that grass and flowers
and trees and people bring
for a flash of time – and then –
and then – make way
for the next glowing light.

Blackbird Cabin
(at Loretto Maryholme)

Inside Blackbird Cabin
I become one of the logs that
make a firm shelter, lying
together, still and sound,
stable and safe. They give
these qualities to me. Here,
silence, not broken by the lapping
of waves outside. Not broken
in the stillness even of
small sounds - inside,
or the chirping of small birds
in trees that brush the walls,
trees that grow and tremble
almost into the cabin itself.

What else will Blackbird Cabin
give me in these days? I wait
to receive...and treasure
the already-gifts of silence,
solitude and heart-warmth,
Light...

Silence. It's the silence
that does it, the silence
that sweeps away the steady thoughts
tumbling through my mind;
the Silence that opens inner doors
otherwise closed against the crashing
waves of thought after thought
after thought.

Inside Blackbird Cabin
the waves and winds
and rain do not disturb
the Silence. They point it out;
they lift it up and I breathe in
its deep peace.

Trees

I watch the trees
take beating after beating-
wind, rain, frost, snow -
and still, and still they move
steadily through their seasons
of fullness, stripping, budding
and allowing their unfolding selves
to emerge like the most elegant
of royalty. Year after year,
they allow the seasons to have
their way, knowing they themselves
will always, always return. Really -
think about it - could it be
any different with us, the most
fragile of creation? Of course
we leave a legacy! Of course
we will return!
Not knowing how or when or in what body
doesn't really matter, does it?

The Driver

Yesterday morning, sitting with tea by the lake,
I met the driver. She is buried
deep within me, hiding all these years
and now- now in the space of slowing down,
she is beginning to show herself
as I have not seen her before. She is
a crying child, abandoned, running for her life,
running from her hiding place, running me.
She is beyond all - frightened, terrified
that to stop running will turn her
into nothingness, lost and abandoned
again.

I open my heart. I open my arms to her,
calling her into them. Tiny steps
are taken; then she runs and hides and
drives me again, from her hidden place.

But a start has been made. I know now
who is driving me, and why.
I soften and breathe deeply and open
my arms again and again and again.

Soon she will come into them
for longer and longer times, and I -
I will be whole again, just as I am,
just as I am, drivenness transformed.

The little one is my teacher and my heart.

A Sudden Shining

The warm tea, heating
both my hands and body at 5am
on this busy summer Saturday
is a settling comfort, along with
the thick, still dark silence.
Now to find the silence within myself
after an unsettling day
and a restless night.

And there is a sudden shining:
find the Silence within.
It is there, buried under
the busyness of summer, of unexpected
guests and delays (like keys locked
in the car at Maryholme yesterday,
waiting two hours for CAA); of necessary
attendance at summer gatherings, and
I realize now, late in life, that
my increasing distaste for summers
is more than heat, humidity and biting insects. It is for
frenzied visitors, invitations,
expectations of social events -
the number growing each year.

Glimpses

And each year now, Silence
calls more and more deeply -
"Let go," she says, "go more slowly, and
"Pay attention. Now is all you have,
all that anybody has."

And so I begin to settle here,
where I am, in this 5am silence, begging Silence
to stay with me, to carry me
through this busy day.

Just As You Are

I am a car, and I have been
stolen by a driver who (how?)
remains hidden from my sight.
This driver races me both forward and
backward, stopping only for gas
and racing me on again. The driver
parks me at night and wakes me
early, so the driving can begin
again - and again - and again.

This driver repeats the takeover
every morning upon waking, and
doesn't stop, except for meals,
all through the day. My body
is inhabited by the driver.

And now - the sudden gift
of sleeping today beyond my
accustomed time - unintentionally,
and the revving of the rushing engine
has stopped me in my tracks:

it is time. It is time to stop.
It is time to hold myself to stopping.
To console. and reassure that lost
and grieving child, always trying
to prove herself worth being seen,
worthy of being loved. Worthy...

Stop now, my frightened crying child.
You are seen. You are held.
You are loved. Just as you are.

Tell the driver as often
as you must until she gets it,
that you are choosing now, and
you are choosing to stop - and step
into the Unknown. You will not
be available for the usual list
that rides you through each day.
The list is lost. The Driver has retired.
You are found.
Found!

The Silence

More and more, the Silence
that surrounds and inhabits all – ALL –
is claiming me – and not just
my attention, but I feel it
sinking into every cell of my body.

My body is becoming the Silence;
Silence is soaking into every cell.

So when I leave the house now –
and often when I am inside it too –
I feel Silence, not as an absence of sound
but as a Presence in itself, a full, thick
Being that fills not only the air, but
everything, everything –
trees and stones, flowers and ground,
animals and insects.
Silence is becoming the air and the ground
and all else, including me, brief visitors
to the planet as we are
and always have been.

Home

Finally, this morning, just now
in the trailer's silent shelter
broken only by soft rain –
a peaceful silence opened
in my chest and spread through
arms, legs, feet and hands…
it is tingling still.

Nothing I could have read
or found or even prayed for
could have offered me, prepared
me for this moment: nothing is ever
darkening except to give Light.

And Light is neither bright nor faint,
neither burning nor cold. Light is
seen and felt in the Heart,
inhabiting the body
like a soft Presence echoing
in a thousand ways:

All is well. Whatever you fear
is dissolving. You are here.
You are here. Light
is present, seen and unseen.
All is well.

Driven

Drivenness, allowing myself
to be driven, mostly unknowingly
and unintentionally, took up residence
in me even before I could talk.

My drivenness showed me
how to be good, so I could escape
beatings. My drivenness won me
scholarships and the highest marks

through all of school. It gave me
a safe path where I was
not safe. But Drivenness is now
tired, wants to stop and can't,
at least not for long.
But just this morning,

I glimpse drivenness
becoming fully tired, even exhausted.
I see her flagging,
unable to keep going as fiercely,
fully, or as long
as she used to with ease.

"How can I give up the keys?"
she says.
"I have never been without them!"
Who will take them? What will
they do?" and behind her cry
is another Voice, tender, soft,
listening, listening with heart, not ears.

"You will lose those keys," she says.
"Better still, you will throw them away.
And I will show you, minute by
minute, even second by second,
the one who has been hidden
since you were born, waiting,
and waiting, for you, only you,
to turn around and see her
and open your arms, so she
can say "You are Home now,
Rest. You are Home."

Not Contradictions

Here I am, sitting in
early morning silence, thick
as a Hudson's Bay blanket,
reading and underlining two
important and sometimes
contradictory books:

Meanwhile, MaCushla is curled
in my lap, head between my breasts,
snoring away.

Something in me laughs!
These are not contradictions
But I don't know how!

Undoing

The silent sun suddenly appears,
filling my eyes with light, stopping me
in my unnecessary movements to keep on
doing, just doing. What else
needs doing? Is the voice of my inner
Voice, and has been as long, as long
as I am alive. But now, now-
I am called a different way. I am called
to stop, to relinquish old ways, to stop
again and again, to listen...
the silence of all trees is the
voice of my call to be, to see, to listen,
To receive...giving has long
been stretched into so little that its ragged edges
disintegrate before my eyes.

Nothing to do, nothing worth doing,
but to listen...

The silent sun suddenly appears,
Filling my eyes with light, stopping me in my
unnecessary movements to keep on
doing, just doing. What else
needs doing? Is the voice of my inner
voice, and has been as long, as long
As I am alive. But now, now-

I am called a different way. I am called
to stop, to relinquish old ways, to stop
Again and again, to listen...
The silence of all trees is the
voice of my call to be, to see, to listen,
To receive...giving has long
been stretched into so little that its ragged edges
disintegrate before my eyes.

Nothing to do, nothing worth doing,
But to listen...

Loons

The loons are leaving –
their cries announce it to the sky.
And I am leaving – finally
taking a next step out of
the fragile building that has
sheltered me all my life,
my eyes, inner and outer,
turned blind to the crumbling
inside me. But now, now

the crumbling can no longer
be denied in myriad ways.
I now see.
The letting go has begun.
The identity has gone long
long ago –

Crying loons are calling me now,
calling me to follow them…

The Presence

Slowly, subtly, the soft evenings
with their fading flowers
are pulling, pulling
at my heart;
sorrow and gratitude,
sorrow and gratitude.
My heart fills with
That Unknown Presence
From whom it all emerges
And goes
And comes again.

Raggedy

If anyone were to ask me how I
feel now, I would have to say –
"I'm feeling raggedy."

Pieces of me are streaming
everywhere, ragged ribbons
of long and struggling years,
trying – oh – never giving up trying –
to find meaning
to contribute to a suffering world,
to help – oh always – to help ---

And now, stopped by quarantine,
by pandemic, by coming up
against a wall of truth I have managed
to evade all my life, I feel –
raggedy. Dissolving, yet also –
surrendered, floating,
Faithful.

Gaze and Wait

Every morning now - a new habit -
MaCushla leads me to the door
going downstairs, facing into
the morning darkness. She loves
to gaze and wait,
gaze and wait, as if showing me
what I can do now that I am
off the highways, the airways
and the long roads weaving back
through my lengthening life.

MaCushla is showing me every day
how to navigate through my inner world:
not turning away from it
not filling time with busyness
not restlessly seeking all manner
of distracting activities, phone calls,
or working through "to do" lists -
but only, only, to gaze and wait.
Gaze and wait. "What you are looking for,"
she seems to say, "is beyond what
your mind can conceive right now. But
it will come. It will come."

The answer, if there is one, is waiting
to present itself. It is not mine
to decide, nor even to seek now -
but to wait. It is on its way to me.
It will present itself with clarity
and grace. My heart vibrates as I
write this - a sure confirmation.

The seeking alone is stretching
my heart open, making a hollow
empty vessel for grace to flow...
ready to receive
ready to receive - whatever is given.

And the seeking is transformed by
MaCushla's patience, her insistence on
purring herself asleep in my arms
every early morning, unable to read
or write as I hold her, insisting that
I gaze and wait, gaze and wait.

Waiting

I have to empty the days
Like a cup of water,
Then lie down
in the bottom of the cup
And wait for, wait in
Trusting anticipation
For whatever will be
Poured over me.

The Heart's Senses

Sometimes, entering into winter means
a flower opening inside the heart
when it cannot open outside,
finished as it is
with earth's flowers –
for now.

Seasons cycle. Earth seasons
are predictable in time; the Heart's
seasons move in their own rhythm –
unfolding briefly, or for a length
of time, then closing again,
only to open unexpectedly.
The Heart
surprises -
in both directions:
gladness, opening; sadness, closing.

Still, the Heart's seasons are
Life's essence, opening and closing
like breathing. And –
like breathing –
they open me into Life itself
And into Love – most of all.

A Sense of Dying

Yes, it's Autumn, and all the trees
are swirling their leaves
to the ground, after they turn
brown and gold on that stalwart trunk.

Branches are now all but empty,
only a few hangers on - soon to be taken
by fierce wind and freezing cold.

Do they have a sense of dying?
Do they release themselves
into that whirling world?
Do they surrender to the wind
and - once released - float
and blow into a previously unknown world?

There is no choice here.
A larger Wind, a stronger Force
follows its own commands, all-
all of it from depths and forces
beyond the considerable but small
human understanding.

Glimpses

We are given
We are taken.
We are blown into
a whirling world; unknown,
unpredictable, and sometimes
but not always unfriendly...

until we open, open arms and hearts
to the wind, unseen and unpredictable,
resting in her unpredictable arms.

Vibrations of Love

When MaCushla lays her nose
in the crook of my left arm,
back feet resting in my left hand,
a sweep - no other word -
a sweep of peace moves
through my body. Nothing,
nothing else is present
in those few minutes, but
a sweep of peace, inhabiting
every cell in in my body -
vibrations of love...

The Tenderness of Trees

Just now, rushing through the freezing air
I felt a reaching out towards me.
Looking up, I saw a small tree,
bottom branches
caught in frozen snow.

This tree's presence called my heart –
"free me, free me," and I felt
a stream of feeling between us –
and turned towards us, seeing
its bottom branches caught
in icy snow. Walking to
the edge of the forest,
I bent and freed
those branches, and felt the relief
of the tree and the one next to it,
freeing that also.

"A simple gesture", you might say,
as I later said to myself, and
"the tree would have waited for a melt –"
all true – all true- but
also true was that moment
of relief in a small
living being – gratitude
sweeping through me –
not mine, but hers.

Stop

And so I am here.
No more working, no more travel,
for months - for many months -
I am wrapped only in
loving companionship, of person,
cat and dog -
of silence, and the sweet presence
of trees - oh, many trees -
and the huge stones, grounding
me, when I cannot ground myself.
Soon, snow will add to the gifts
with its special silence and
shared settling of the world.

How much I have been given
in my lifetime! How freely
offered all I need to balance
the necessary struggle with
the painful lives of others!
My whole life is a gift -
Stopping wraps it in layers -
of knowing, remembering, receiving.
receiving.

Stopping

All my life I have been
riding on a fast moving train -
on and off - mostly on -
and now the train won't stop
and I know nothing else.

Stopping makes my heart
beat faster, not slower,
opens a gushing stream
higher into the air. Stopping
opens wounds I didn't even know
inhabited my heart.

Tears rise, spreading through
my whole body like a rush of
realizing what I didn't know I knew.

Loosen, soften, surrender -
these are the tears that are
taking me home.

Life's Spiral: Giving Gold

And now, and now -
Life's spiral is winding around,
collecting years of bright strands,
braiding them together in
sorrow and beauty. How
visibly, heartfully stunning
is one life! Any life -
All life.

Yesterday I came upon
a dying beetle on the road's edge.
He/she was still moving
the tiniest of legs and wings,
but barely. I held the
shining body until they all stopped,
praising and thanking him
for his time in the world.
Then I laid him reverently
on the freezing grass
and walked on, filled with
a vibrating stream of connecting
to everything, everything, even
the tiniest of creatures
in this amazing amazing world.
Amazing and breathstopping, really -

Just to look. Just to feel
the strands weaving us
all, all- not just humans -
but every miniscule of creation -
all into one. We ARE one!
No separation exists, except
in the human's limited
imagination and small seeing.

Thanks to the beetle.
Thanks to every blade of grass
and tiny pine needle. Thanks, to
every fallen leaf, giving gold.
And all, and all that my eyes
can see - and especially -
all they do not see.

I am not mine any more.
Life's Spiral is claiming me,
and I sink into her arms
in grateful relief.

The Spiral of Life has arms
and heart big enough for us all.

Falling Away

Everything I have loved all my life -
reading, writing, painting, coloring,
traveling, visiting, being visited -
it is all, all falling away.

A warm enveloping silence - like
arms wrapping around me -
is taking its place. A Grand
Silence, thick and warm,
calling and calling when
I don't respond soon enough.
Perhaps it is also the call of
the child standing in the crib,
alone in the dark, giving up her
beaten, crying self.

If so, then a step into Light
is happening. If so, then
she finally knows that
all is well, all is well, and all
will continue to be well, as I
welcome and hold her and -
most important of all, comfort her
for the rest of my living days.

And then perhaps she will
be waiting for me on the other side,
arms open and reaching,
as I always see her inside
my own heart.

And I will go into them.

I will finally go into them.

And all else, all else
will fall away.

The Line of Time

Under the line of Time
Light prevails. Her streams
softly flowing, arms wrapping
and holding, comforting and
releasing. "It's time."
Her time. Only time.

Let go of reading, let go
of lists to do. Let go
of expectations – your own
and others of you.

Open – that's all it takes –
open and release. Receive –
receive and realize that
no matter how long it takes
words no longer work –

that sitting in silence
whether dark or light, without
expectation, wondering
or words, opens the world
both inner and outer, where
you are a small twinkling light
of presence and grace.

No judging or wondering,
No measuring or examining,
Only Presence,
Silent and full of Light.

Searching has ended;
Being has stepped into her place.

Let it all go – Meaning
Has gone out with the tide.
Presence – cleansing and
Constant – lives now,
Lives Now,
in your inmost heart.

Mahti (Little Bear)

Her eyes find you first.
Huge and brown,
soft and pleading,
longing for love, both
receiving and giving.

She is an orphan dog, brought
to us from the far north, choosing us
almost before we chose her.
She is chosen; so are we.
And her fierce love,
desperate even in her often
loud barking, is her
faithful presence, begging
not to be left alone too long.

Goodness and desperate being
shine, actually shine
from Mahti,
a daily gift of furry, faithful love.

We are found by her eyes.

Stones of Invitation

The Stones that once were
Stones of Consolation have now become
Stones of Invitation – calling me out of
my too busy life; "away, away"
they now cry daily, especially
as I pass them on the morning walk,
every day, every day.

And what are they
inviting me to? Their steady, solid
peace is the first thing –
their solid presence
through every season. In
this late fall, they are
covered with fallen leaves
and snow. And yet they call
as I pass, and yesterday
I went to them, and found
solace in their solid corners,
felt held in their unwavering arms,
knew trust and care for those
few minutes, enough to sustain me
for the day. And what, what
are they sustaining me through?

They know – more than I do –
More deeply than I can imagine –
the grief that mirrors in me
their large, solid, unmovable being.

They know, more than I do –
the approach of life's completion.
They know – more than I do –
the great gifts I have been given
all my life, that will never leave,
but have already begun to fade.

And yet – yet all is not lost. Is
never lost! Instead, it is held
in the deep earth, in the wide world –
and in the Stones of Invitation
to Consolation!

A Bouquet of Grace

Silence begins and ends the day –
and now, now – it appears in times
between the beginning and ending. Small
moments – while walking or
pondering what to do next, or
turning within for a brief moment,
and finding – finding – mainly
Silence.

Life's necessities and even
daily details are falling away, though –
thank God – not all and not always.
The crackling morning fire sings
more presence than human words.

And Life's fullness, diminishing
in detail, is opening in depth and
a fullness of completion, a
bouquet of grace. Never in my life
have I been as fully, magically
present to the fullness of reality, to
what-is-here-now: wind, cold, snow;
the trees' stillness, the road's emptiness.
And more, Oh- so much more –
as if what is seen is a doorway
to the Unseen, even fuller and deeper
than the Seen Itself.

What stunning gifts! And all, all
of them, opening windows into
the usually unseen Fullness
of Life in every moment.

And every moment we are all,
All being offered a
Bouquet of Shining grace.

The River

"The River is Flowing
Home to the Sea"
writes Carolyn McDade,
and so it sings itself in me…
now, when I look at the river
flowing past our house, where
I have lived for all these years,
my heart sings with the knowing
that this river, this very river flowing
past our house, where I have lived for
all these years,
my heart sings with the knowing
that this river, this very water
might well someday
reach the sea, and eventually
move far enough East
as to wash upon the shores,
or at least brush against
my native ground.

Looking at the river, my heart
Swells with gratitude and grace.
I might not see Newfoundland, but
the river will bring my heart there and –
really – in this way –
I will still go home.

Whirling Grace

Today I visited with the wind –
that messenger of whirling grace –
stood among her arms and breath
cleansing the world.
These past few days she has
been voracious, even vicious,
stripping dead branches, swaying
decades-old trees, whipping
calm lakes into waves and foam,
coming to the edge of destruction.

And thus the wind visits
from time to time,
but not predictably. She doesn't send
an email or a phone call, asking
permission or hospitality. She
arrives, often with little warning,
and cleanses the world.

And I – I sometimes hold my breath,
Waiting to see what will go next
And whether – like the wind –
I can let it go,
releasing my own life.

A Smoothing

Waves of pain wash though me
like a tide, like a pounding sea,
beating over rocks, long in place
and staying there, solid and secure.

Yet the waves persist, and will
always persist, oceans of
presence and cleansing, of
releasing and surrendering.

They pass, but not before
their work of softening and
loosening - a smoothing, really,
is done for another day.

Grief grows as it must and will;
it is the necessary cleanser
of all that went before, the weaver
of what is real. Not to be denied
or ignored, or the grounding foundation
that grief brings is lost forever.

Grief is the softening -
the necessary cleanser of all
that went before, the one wave -

the journey has begun.

Tree

I wish I were a tree, whose roots
go deep, tangling and tingling
with life energies of other trees, trees
I don't know and will never know
and don't need to know. Standing
still, I am already fed, always fed,
with the silence and storms
of the forest.

All I do - or ever need to do - is stand
still, allowing myself to be buffeted, even
broken, by the visits of wind and snow
and rain, and even humans, with their
saws and knives, cutting out parts of me,
shutting down other parts. All the while

my roots remain, will always remain,
long after my upper body
becomes the earth again.

Claimed

The quiet has claimed me.

No longer do I claim
the early morning silence; it
has claimed me. No longer
do I write or even read
during that blessed time.

No–I sit and watch the wood fire,
feeling those eager flames
dance for me - a reassurance.
I sit and feel wrapped -
as I just was in bed, in
silence and stillness.

Perhaps they are the most
sacred of words: silence, stillness.
Not just to speak them, but to
feel them stirring within. Silence
and stillness...they bring comforting
peace and a fulness of possibility,
all at once.

Later, I walk into the forest,
trees rooted and solid, even
the youngest and smallest.
When the daily world is filled
with movement and noise, trees
hold space, contain silence,
holding the world together
in hidden embrace. I have only
to step into them to be claimed.
They welcome me as one
of their own, whenever I
stand still among them.

Light

Light can hardly be seen
Yet it is there, still there,
always there -

tingling the body
calling the soul
opening closed places
comforting dark corners.

Light is always there

Unknowing

I have descended into the Cloud
of Unknowing – an old phrase,
to be sure, but after all the years –
a lifetime – of knowing, of pursuing
knowing, of making a life dedicated
to knowing – Unknowing
has opened herself like a soft
blanket, wrapping herself
around me with tenderness –

"It is all enough," she whispers
as I sink into her tender arms.
"All enough. Just sit here, in
this soft blanket of silence
and darkness. All is well. All
will continue to be well, no matter
what happens – no matter –

So I sink into her blanket,
warm and held. Warm and held
and surrendering all I thought
I knew for something greater:
Unknowing: the height
and depth and soft certainty
of enough.
Enough.

Stars

Standing outside in the silent night
darkness wrapping the world,
stars call as clearly as bells.
My neck strains to look up,
to keep looking up in wonder
at the small bright openings into
another world.

Stars bring silence like a
warm winter coat. Stillness
invites a wrapping round, a holding
as comforting as a woolen blanket
or a warm bath. What else
is there to this life,
except the comfort of the night sky
and the stars call, that Silence
opening into a larger world
than I can ever comprehend?

The Day Came

And then the day came
when I couldn't read or write
at all, so full was my mind
in the dark thick silence
of pre-dawn, but only sit,
eyes closed, body tingling,
breathing in and out –
Life's essence.
And in that pre-dawn stillness
I knew my life to be complete, except
For what Silence and Stillness
give to the world, healing agents
of peace, where there is so little.
Even "The Cloud of Unknowing"
couldn't claim me. I no longer
need to read it: I was in it,
wrapped in it, floating
in a sea of emptiness, nothing,
nothing else in sight, all else
in a different realm of life's
necessities. There and not there.

The depths claim me. My real
Home, to which – someday –
I will return forever...
Unknowing, Knowing
All.

A Peak

Everything reaches a peak: a person,
Any given area, even a country –
And now, in our time, the world
we knew – in every way –
the world we knew is dissolving
before our eyes, demanding
the necessary changes it is
unfurling, bringing about.

The Peak has been reached.

And now – transformation
once again rises from ashes
and waste, from fear and
desperation, from
disorienting dilemmas…

The climb to a new peak
is only barely,
barely begun.

The Fire

At 6am, the fire is burning
brightly, eagerly, almost dancing
in its eagerness to give heat
and the brightest light. All
it needs is the attention of
wood, of hands offering it
the food of kindling
and small logs. Then,
heat and light are eagerly,
generously offered, filling
the house with living comfort.

And that's what the wood fire
offers: living comfort, and
the invitation to attend, attend,
no clearer reminder of the
necessity – yes – necessity- of
attending to the inner fire,
burning as fiercely as the
outer one, and needing, claiming
similar attention, so that inner fire
can burn as fiercely, and open
her soul to warm the world.

Suddenly

Suddenly, I became present –
a fullness of soul rising through layers –
and embracing heart and body,
firmly planting me in the place
where I have lived for decades
without fully claiming.

I belong here now – as deeply
and as rooted as one of the trees
that surround me, and as flowing
as the river that runs – rising
and falling –
not far from the back door.

How I got here is a strange
and difficult and lovely mystery – but
isn't every mystery defined by those words?
Isn't every life ever lived?

Opening

My soul has opened:
nothing else will go through
my mind, except the Great Light,
even outshining (most of the time)
the Darkness that appears, though
less often now, less often.

Letting all be.
Letting all come and go
as it does anyway – I
give up the fight – I give
up the expectations –

I live through my soul's
Opening. Transformation
appears.

Taken

Something has fallen away.
Life's layers are clearer, haloes
Around unknown heads, holding
Sacred space...I am one, only
One, and relieved to be so.

I release my spiritual hunger, full
Now, and needing nothing more
But a contented waiting
For the greatest Unknown
to claim me, my arms opened
To be taken, my breath the heavy
Sighs of great relief.
I have given all I can, loved in
Great leaps. Now I raise my arms
In relieved surrender: not to
Go further, but to be led further-
Taken.
(Christmas 2022)

Spark

A burning has begun in me –
Old words, written long ago,
shock me with their new meaning.
I could not have understood then
what I was implying, or even
meaning: now, the spark
that appeared then – opening
the light to write those words
has fanned into a flame. And
who knows how strong the flame
will grow? Or how large?
Certainly, it is consuming me
Now, in ways I could not
know then, though
the words poured themselves
out of me anyway. Anyway –
not only have I received
a spark, now bursting into flame –
I am becoming a fire
in these final years of life,
and fan it I must.
Fan it I must.

Whatever Life...

This fierce and feisty cat, lying
On her back in my arms
this early morning chooses
her life. Every move. When
she will eat, when she
will refuse food or even a tender
touch; when she wishes to
go outside and when she will
come in; when she will groom
or curl into a ball for solid sleep.
The back of my fingers
traces her under-chin,
as she offers her throat to me.

Every day I become more and
more aware of how – in her (so-called)
small world, she determines
the details of her life, choosing
and refusing – even food – certainly
when she will go outside and come in,
and when she wants comfort – or not.

MaCushla is a model for
how to live whatever life it is
you are living, I am living.

In her small and catlike ways,
Her necessities and choices,
She rules her own life,
As far as is possible. Watch her.
Then she opens to what is –
what is – and lives from there.

Beautiful Friend

When Mahti, our dog,
Stands behind me, and emits
a sudden loud bark, my skin shifts
and my heart pounds. It is
a fright that takes time
to settle – even when I know
that she means nothing,
nothing by it except to ask
for food, as dogs do.

But every time, every time
that bark shifts my heart, and it takes
time for my heart to settle and
my breath to return. It is not
her fault, dear affectionate friend
that she is; not her fault
but a medication given her
to help something worse…

anyway – it is the fright
in me that is to be calmed,
while I turn and rub the head
of our beautiful friend Mahti.

Inner Flames

Reading through my doctoral thesis
for the first time in twenty years,
and even my own published poetry,
a small spark that – I suppose now –
has lived buried in my heart
for twenty years – leaps into flame.

Really? Did I write that? Did I
even know that, so long ago?
Where did it go? How did I lose it?

But now matter now. Now, it
is here – the vision I had all those years
ago, for which I was vilified and rejected,
and – at best – ignored and misunderstood.

And isn't that the path, I see
Only now? Aren't those the
birthing pains of labour? What mother
gives birth without pain?

But I could not see anything
birthed by my vision, by my
shared seeing, ignored and vilified.

Glimpses

Perhaps it is only now, only now
that the small flame igniting
the larger one until it was shut down,
can show its light again.
I see it, I welcome it. I am
thankful, even with the pain,
for all it opened for me, to me,
into the life – inner and outer –
I live now.

Part II

Still

We are today in the calm
before the storm that has announced
its coming. Small breezes flap
the flags outside in the morning
darkness. All else is still. Still…
only the crackling fire speaks
its small sounds this December morning.

Where do we go from here? Is
always, the question –
yet, an unanswerable one.
Better would be: what is here.
now, now in this moment?
Stay there. There – in the
thick silence, the crackling fire,
the morning blanket of darkness.
The Stillness.
All else, everything else in the world
Will emerge from these.
Stay there.

Morning Stillness

In the dark morning stillness
A whole world becomes present.
The day's possibilities – as well as
necessities (today, snow clearing)
open up with the slow dawning
light – giving time for both
consideration and necessity
to join hands.

What privilege it is to sit
in this deep morning silence
wrapping me like a blanket
before this day's demands
begin tugging at mind
and heart! What gift and
grace, what shining path I am given
to walk into this day, no
matter the requirements!

Morning stillness sets the stage
for a day's surprise emergence!

Coasting Down the Hill

When I was a child, we eagerly
waited for snow enough to slide
down the hills surrounding us
everywhere, but especially those
we could slide down on our
ancient sleds, belly down, gaining
speed as we went. It was the normal
treat of winter in those early days,
waited for, anticipated with eager joy,
and a cleaned up sled.

Remembering this so vividly, I am
this morning realizing that I am
indeed casting now, down the hill
of my own life, belly down, snow
in my face, energy diminishing
while the sled goes faster and
faster as the hill steepens.
And realizing – perhaps for the
first time – that I will not
be climbing back up the hill
as I did at eight or ten –
that this casting keeps going,
even building its momentum
of a downward slide…

Still, every hill ends
at a level bottom. Every hill
stops somewhere. Where will mine
be? The shining grace, growing
each day, holds that knowing,
not I. I continue to coast, until
Home, with its lighted windows,
appears – a beacon of welcome,
and the relief of stopping.

Doesn't Know

The forest doesn't know that
it's Christmas Day.
Neither do the birds, wisely
sheltering in their carefully-built
nests, nor the animals, better prepared
than many humans, to stay in their cozy
burrows, ready with food and warmth.

And then there are the trees, roots
so deep in the ground that their
nourishment never ends, and is
shared among them all.
"Who are these bustling creatures?"
they wonder, "unprepared for anything
except their own wishes, which
don't often come to pass?" Weather
prevails. Weather determines movement
and journeys, homestays and relinquishment,
not humans, poor innocent creatures!"

And so today, Christmas Day, opens
and invites everyone and everything
to be still, to listen and receive,
to be transformed by the great
gifts of the universe hidden
in snowflakes and wind.

Stop. Be Still. Receive the world.

Alive! Alive!

On this last day of a
pandemic year, having
lived through three years of
quarantine, masks, fear
of one another in public
places, family violence (daily
reports), shortages of food
in supermarkets, and – covering all –
constant news of wars in so
many parts of the world –

A turning of the year
comes down to this:
a contented cat, purring
in my arms, breathing on my heart;
a warm house, safe in deep winter,
a loving dog, eager to please,
and a strong heartful woman,
able and eager to sustain it all…

While I sit here in the dark
early morning on the edge of light,
in my familiar warm old blanket of silence,
marvelling at the grace and blessing
of being alive, just being alive!

II.

Everything here has its day —
its flowering and its fading.
Sometimes an ending is
barely noticed, or only decades
later, or perhaps not at all.

But noticing is not the point
and never was. Never was.
Noticing is the icing on the cake,
but not every cake needs icing…

The world I knew is fading
now, just this way, having
offered and given a richness
only to be recognized long after
it's gone, like all former
years in their thousands!

III.

But what privilege, what
joy and gratitude; what
grace to be alive in this world!
To be swept into the Great
Unknown, into Light and Dark,
into the long Unfolding,
forever a part of the Unknown
Herself, more than the Known.

Alive! Alive! to the last
breath! And then –
sliding over into
the arms of all the loved ones,
known and unknown,
who have already stepped
through that thin veil.

Still: alive! Alive!

Time Now...

Is it time now, to stop?
Stop searching, stop looking
for connection, inner peace, light
for the hours of every day
to be full and satisfying? Is it
time now to simply open, receive,
what is already there, waiting,
a Great Inner Light, just
on the edge of my heart's small
boundaries, waiting for me to
remove those separating lines
so – so it can flow in,
filling me with all I have been
searching for, all my life,
All My Life – and now – now –
the search is no longer
mine to do.

It is Time Now just
to receive, receive, opening
that searching heart like
closed fists whose fingers
are now, finally –
slowly, tentatively, longingly
opening, opening –

and Light IS flowing in,
sometimes streaming, blinding
me with amazement,
and
removing all my resistance
and ignorance really,
filling me to overflowing
with peace, with the
unspeakable, indescribable
LIGHT that is LOVE –
the Love that fills the world,
that grows trees and plants, animals
and thoughts and people,
the Love that powers oceans
and rivers and food from the earth.

Time now, Time now to open
my small heart…and receive, receive.

Waters of Grace

Slowly, subtly, I am being stripped
of everything, everything – now
even my morning time, stripped
of the joy of reading and writing
in the deepest silence – with MaCushla
taking up residence
in my arms, snuggling her nose
in the crook of my arm.

And yesterday, my last group
of women sent not a single response –
not one of them – to my decision
to cancel their group meetings
altogether. Altogether –

So – the messages are clearer
than they every were, and now –
now I see, still with half-covered eyes –
I see coming the changes
I would not choose, being
chosen for me. They are
coming clearer, rising from
an ocean's bottom
through the waters of grace.

Let me see. Let me accept.
Let me – another unfamiliar
part of me – become visible
and embraced, a full heart
releasing all else, carried,
carried as never before –
releasing, releasing.

Stirring of the World

Even the smallest stirring
shakes and shimmers what once
was dependable, predictable,
comforting. Then it shifts,
and not just in small things:
schedules, family, friends,
work directions, even weather –
and now, after seventy-five
years, the shift is deepening,
affecting planet-sized stirrings –
wars and weather, travel and
time. A major adjustment
is at hand…is here.
Discomfort, unpredictability,
revoked decisions and
unexpected news on small
and large scales –
these are the order of the day.

The world is stirring – shaking
up usual structures and frameworks,
all falling apart together,
while we –
depending on them for lifetimes –
dissolve and fall into the
stirring, helpless and holding on…

and letting go…
letting go.

Falling Apart

Even as Light itself lengthens
at this time of year,
darkness prevails in the world:
wars, wars and rumours of wars
dominate in the frequent, repetitive
daily news. Homes bombed,
people shifting
to other countries, where
their language is not even
spoken…

Ignorance prevails,
even in our so-called "peaceful"
countries, those "governing"
showing off nothing but
self-ignorance and self-focused
grasping for money and power.
What happened
what happened
to government for the people?
What happened to
serving the people, to
the country itself?

All that we in the world now
treasured
appreciated
counted on –
has become a
precarious edge, cracked open,
the crack widening
instead of closing,
a future
still unravelling.

Tender Moments

Most valuable of all moments
are the tender ones – as heart melts,
as body tingles, as the moment –
whatever in that moment – opens
the heart's door, softening it in
tender tears, or shifts of seeing,
or even momentary visions.

And not to think – no – never
to think – that such moments
are special to some special
people – no – they are there
for every single person. They
are the moments we walk through,
swim through, work through, cry
through, rage through –
all moments,
all moments hold that small
sometimes invisible opening that
is always there.
Always there.

Look to your own tenderness. Stay
with it, in it, as long as you can.
It will open you to see the
soft love in every miniscule moment
of your own world. It will
save you.

Opening Arms

Coming into my own life now
muscles I didn't know were tight
are loosening, even relaxing.

Space, inner and outer,
is appearing. Not
scheduled, even not practiced –
but arising
like a small spark hidden inside
all these decades, hidden
and waiting, now breathed into
a Larger Presence
of emptiness, fullness and Light.
I glimpse it and feel it
becoming familiar, even when –
unconsciously – I return
(but only for a moment)
to the old way of rushing and
"getting everything in" and
checking off a list.

No more.

My arms are open to receive
a Light always present,
always ready to wrap me
in Peace.

If I choose. If I choose.

Forgetting/Remembering Everything

Reading my own poems now
every morning
sitting in the dark silence,
MaCushla burrowing
into the elbow of my left arm –

I am deeply moved – perhaps
"shattered" is the better word –
by what I was writing nearly
a decade ago – about endings,
about diminishing energy
and the ending of work –
and yet, and yet –
in the face even of that
knowing, so many years ago –

I plunged forth and worked
Even harder, forgetting
(or denying) what I already
knew, already had been shown.
But now –
years later, I read those revelations
as prophecies I recognized
but could not (or would not)
embody, so – my body –
that temple of God – did it
for me. Stopping me now
in my hurrying tracks –

Perhaps it's the body who is
the ultimate teacher, who
decides everything about one's
place in the world. That gift –
one's body – with its subtle
differences and simultaneous
sameness for every human
walking and has ever walked
this earth – my body,
like everyone and everything
that has ever known life,
ever lived in any way or form –
decides the what
and when of life
and death.

What consolation those words
bring! What invitation
for surrender! What
release into the Whole,
letting go of the particular –

and falling into waiting
arms, leaning into the
Heartbeat of the Universe,
and releasing, surrendering
everything.

Everything.

The Only Light

Sitting in the darkness just
before dawn, I release my lifelong
need to think and plan, to organize
and schedule for the sake of safety.

This has been my dependable path
since I was ten. It carried me profoundly,
beautifully, and is gently leaving me now,
reminding me with a gentle push
into deeper emptiness that
Life is Larger, Deeper, Grander
than fixed schedules, rewarding
though they be. Instead, the sky opens,
and in the vast darkness
one bright shining star
stops my breathing. Nothing else,
nothing in that moment matters
as this One Light in deepest darkness.

This is the Light that is calling me home,
the only Light - no thought or image, no
poem, or words of any kind -
the Only Light calling me home.

Dark Light

Before Light there is always Darkness:
doesn't the day – every day – announce
this faithfully, without fail? Light
takes us through the day, every day,
but Darkness is just as faithful
and brings its own settling,
its own
Dark Light.

Inside that Dark Light, Silence
illumines a deeper world, a world
that opens a heart beyond
imagining. The presence of darkness
is a gift of Mystery, both
inside and out
in its rhythm and Grace.

Light and Dark: both
full of grace. But the
Presence of Darkness opens
a way to the wrapping
of a Light that contains both.

Chosen

Is it the bug bites, forcing me
into helpless irritation of skin,
of voice, even of heart? If so,
Quaking, I welcome the push,
the inescapable passage
from old ways to new, not - NOT-
deliberately or even knowingly
chosen. I am chosen.
I am not choosing this. The only thing
I can choose is to accept
or to keep fighting - everything -
and, God help me, against all
the tears of my tormented self,
I choose this exact moment. I choose
acceptance of what is given,
though I am not giving it to myself.

Always Held

There is only this: really
only this: the thick presence
of Silence, holding all;
sounds of morning - birds,
boiling kettle, dehumidifier -
all held. Always held.

To you O Silence, I turn
now, again, again -
and finally - deeper and
deeper, marvelling at depths
I never knew you had, depths
you held until I was ready
to be held.

Steady Ground

Two women - one, ninety three,
the other ninety-four*
are the steady ground for me
in these otherwise strange days,
replete with unexpected schedules
and interrupted plans
and unpredictable interventions -
enough of that.

Pandemic life is hard enough,
but these two women,
stalwart and steady in daily presence
even in their worried times
are, I begin to see -
pegs in the ground of my otherwise
flapping tent. But there is one more,
with whom I live, who is daily,
blessedly, the steadiest ground
of all.

S. Loretta Dower and Aunt Bride.

All Light
(for Elizabeth Davis' birthday, 2021)

And so the Hidden unfolding
that has been happening all this time -
years and years and years -
rises to an inner surface
just on the edge of visible.

And it is all light. All Light.

The struggles, the suffering,
the judgments, the wishes
that things were different -
all transformed into these strong
streams of Light, wrapping in
one another like strands
of ribbon, like offerings of grace.

Everything, everything - not a thing
omitted - mosquitoes and spiders
along with flowers and trees -
all that aggravates along with
unspeakable beauty - All Light.

Here in this moment, even though
a minute from now it will be otherwise -
Here, now, all is unfolding,
has unfolded, as the Grace of Being
designed it so. All Good.
All Good.

Open arms. Welcome Light.
Surrender to the gifts
flowing like a waterfall
into your tender, delicate heart
hidden in the bushes
of daily demands, felt concerns,
anxiety and fatigue.

They cannot overcome, and
they will never darken
the Light that burns in your Heart.

Rhythm

One day follows the next like
a chain of beads (some would say
Rosary beads, but not all)-
held together by dark and light,
dark and light - the rhythm
of our earth world.

In the same way, Love unfolds,
deepens, creating an anchor
unmovable, though its rhythms
might cause the the inexperienced
to question its truth, this love -
No -

Earth, sky, sun, moon, stars -
these our only teachers, guides
of wisdom: a rhythm of sweet
darkness and tender light
in mind and heart and world!

I Don't Know

I don't know how I knew
when it was time to work less
and be present, just present,
more.

I don't know how I knew
that I had to get up at 5am
to listen, to read, to write
my life: just that.

I don't know how I knew
when it was time to stop reading,
just stop - and listen, just listen
to thick darkness, that silent
Presence, and that inner
wordless welcoming.

I don't know how I knew
that seeing one raindrop
land on a leaf and announce
its presence is more important
than any words I might speak,
read or write.

I don't know how I knew
that only poems - my own
and a few others - made
any sense at all, or all the sense
that words could make
in this world.

I don't know how I knew -
only that one day, one morning
I woke up and knew. And sat
receiving in the dark before dawn
not words, but a Presence,
the Presence of Light itself.

Return

Where is this place called peace?
As long as I can remember
I've searched for it, longed for it,
felt it touch me like a game of tag
and then it was gone again. I look
and look and then suddenly remember-
Peace comes to me. I do not decide.

And where is this place called Love?
Oh how I long to live there! All
my life, Love too has visited
me often, but never stayed as
I hoped it would...or it changed forms
and I lost sight of it for awhile.

Yet, here I am in Elder Wisdom,
standing with open arms and bruised old heart,
always waiting to welcome them both,
even knowing they will leave again.
But now I know, now I really know,
they'll always return. Return.

Six Ducks

Six ducks are swimming together
on the large long waters
of Lake Simcoe. As I watch
first one, then another
glides into leading the rest.
One falls behind, another
draws up alongside; they
are constantly changing places.
Now they stretch out
into one long line, each one
by herself, but in sight
of all the rest.

And isn't that the very way
we too glide through our lives?
First with one, then another,
then alone, but always in sight
of those we know, those
who come, and yes - even
those who go from our lives?

All the same. We are all
the same, every spark
of every created creature -
we come and we go, first with one,
then another, and others.

The whole created world is visible
and held in six ducks, cruising
quietly in Lake Simcoe.

II.

All day they glide,
smoothly it seems, across
the lake's surface
matching their smoothness,
but beneath, just beneath
that still cover
little feet are scrabbling,
moving quickly, propellers of motion.

And isn't it so with us too?
We talk, we move, we enter
in lines in the bank or the grocery store,
standing more-or-less still, while
all the while our minds
are chattering away, going
from one topic to the next,
one judgment to the next -

until stillness, inner stillness,
cannot find space to breathe us
among so much unceasing activity.

Until we choose -ah -
there's the turning point -
until we turn, again, within, again
and again and again,
calming the voices,
choosing the stillness.

III.

But this is no achievement.
This is no goal to be reached,
so that we will never have to
engage the struggle again.

This is a practice, with no
achievement - only the patient
faithfulness, the loving forgiveness
of ourselves, again, again and again.
Then again, until we stand,
finally, before the Light
that awaits us, and we open
our arms, stepping - oh so
confidently, oh so eagerly -
into the arms that await us.

Stop and Wait

The inner world does not – repeat –
does not resonate with the outer.
That slippery insight, that inner
shifting, owns its own path, and
widens and narrows by its own
light and dark, light and dark,
not dictated by the vagaries
of weather or conversation
or time of day or time of year or…

Instead, as in just now, after
days of inner darkness and lament,
a Light appeared, opening into
a Loosening, a widening of
something I didn't know was
tight and narrow…but only
felt it, felt it. Now, the day
opens: the world opens, my
soul opens. Until it all decides
(not "I decide") to close it again.
What Great Light decides this?
What unfathomable truth?
What Maker of the world?

Whatever the name – and there are
many – in this moment,
it has opened in me, and
my soul is content,
bathed in Light.

Burning

Open a moment – and burning begins.
inner burning, that is: the heart
beats and burns, opening doors
kept closed during ordinary day tasks –
during noise and conversation –

but always, always, the sanctuary
lamp stays lighted, burning in
the inmost heart. Claim it –
claim the burning flame of
stillness, of sanctuary – be
in retreat from life's demands,
steady noise and machines-
over and over, many times a day –
in retreat, in sanctuary.

In that sanctuary stillness
your life will return, will
renew that small burning flame
that is your true life – your
heart life, your soul life.

Breaking the Habit

My long escape from my own life
has been doing and getting done –
lists upon lists upon what
needs to be done, should be done,
could be done. When time
stretches out with lists
becoming shorter, I find ways
to lengthen them. Over many years
life became lists: stopping
a torment, even with meditation.

Who am I without something
to be done? I never thought to ask –
until now.

Now, the habit of lists
is falling away. Some rising
inner spaciousness is claiming
me now, day by day, overriding
the lists, the importance of lists,
the crossing off satisfaction
of getting done what is on a list.

What a strange and unfamiliar
feeling! Like being wrapped
in a warm blanket, all
the doings floating around
but none firmly fixed –
only the warm blanket
fills and firms the space – though
full comfort is still a ways off.

I settle into its wrapping:
the hold of doing is shattering-
breaking into more pieces daily.

The presence of trees and birds,
and the silence of snow
fills me to overflowing, when
I open – empty,
empty,
empty
of tasks.

Welcoming...

Life journeys are shaped
as much by the negative as by
the positive strands, weaving through
our lives, through
our soul's journeys –

negative ones open new directions,
unimagined while dancing in the
blinding light of the positive...

they are weavers, really, offering
a garment of such strength and
beauty that – without both, the
garment weakens and fades away.

But when arms and heart
open to welcome both dark and light,
warm with knowing and the soul's
full vision, a peace not
anticipated, imagined, or even
understood, fills the soul,
opening the heart
in surrender and swirling,
settling peace. Even if
(as it usually is)

only for a few moments.

It is enough. It is truly enough.

Revelation

Nature has become my tabernacle –
I haven't seen it until now –
forest, skies, rivers – and all – all
the many animals wandering through –
fox, rabbit, raven and crow –
birds in their multiple forms –
even bear and lynx and weasel,
wolf and coyote –

they are all sacred presences
on this failing earth. They are all
signs – no- more than signs –
they are – are – manifestations
of the Divine Herself, in
whose womb we all together
live and grow and have our being.

And the Silence wraps them all –
holds them in her nourishing blanket,
including me, including anyone
who opens or doesn't to the flow
of Earth's unfolding in all, all
the many revelations
of Her Divine Presence.

And meanwhile, moon and stars
and sun herself, in darkness and
light, play the Earth's rhythms
on a soft drum, always
calling us – the wanderers,
the seekers –
the never-enoughs-
home to the heart of it all-

Home to the Heart, without
a moment's stopping.

Glance of Heaven

Suddenly, sitting at the kitchen table
in early morning darkness,
I was swept through
with a wonder of being alive.

Thought disappeared. Plans disappeared.
It was this moment – this moment alone –
feeling MaCushla's weight in my arms,
hearing the crackling fire,
seeing the thick darkness outside-
feeling feet tingling –
all of it somehow vibrated,
vibrated alive, thickened even,
with the astounding aliveness,
the stunning beauty
of this moment, never to come
again. *I saw it*!

What gift! What Grace!
This glance of heaven!

Making Way

And now, I claim myself.
not by what I do or who
loves me, or what I have achieved
in a lifetime – none of these.
Already, already they are fading.
Even I am surprised by all
I have done and written,
travelled and taught. It is
all past now, and the results
are not mine, but belong
to those who received them.

I, sit here in the dark
before dawn in wonder and thanks,
knowing the completion that
is already arriving, that is
already here –

A comforting heat comes
from the wood stove, warmth
filling the cold house on this
midwinter morning – and it
is because the wood is burning
and will soon be nothing
but coals and ashes. It's
heat has a limit, and so
has the life of everyone,
everything. But how
wondrous, how astounding
and precious it is to know

to fully realize, that every
life contributes to the life
emerging, be it
grass or snow or human
being. We each in our turn
make way for whoever,
whatever or however
this magnificent world
shoots life into the universe.

Each and all, we make way…
We make way…

Heart's Companion

Thank you, God, for sending me
MaCushla.
She keeps my heart open and alive.
She evokes love in my being.

She makes me smile many times
a day, and sometimes reminds
me of how quickly
I become impatient –

But always, all day and night,
she is a messenger of love.
She demands back rubs often –
demands –
bringing me to my knees to do them,
while she warms my knees at night.

She follows me often – through
the house, and in her brief daily
tree visits in the snow.
When snow is gone, I walk with her
on a leash.
MaCushla – heart's companion.

Alive, Alive!

Finally, words fell away –
books piled up, none of them
holding any interest to draw me –
even my own. It is
a sense of dissolving, of
melting, of fullness
in a new way: presence.

Presence to whom or what
did not make itself known.
It was only Presence itself
moving through my body,
beginning
with my feet, alive with a
light of energy, of vibration,
of heat in waves,
a tide of being alive.

And within – everything
left me – my books, my words –
only my breath and the gentle
vibrations sweeping through my body
announcing "Alive! Alive!"

Portal

Someday, the Silence will
claim you altogether, even as
she opens your heart now,
more and more deeply – settling
and expanding you all at once.

You will (as sometimes
happens now) surrender
and be wrapped and carried
by her, in her,
knowing at last the fullness
of Being you have sought
all your life. All your whole life.

The gift will be given fully
and you will receive its fullness
just as you receive with awe
the small, vivid moments
of it now. A portal has
opened, and will not be
closed – only deepened
and lengthened,

bringing you home.

The Real Treasure

Yesterday I visited an old professor
whose life had been given to poetry,
and now- decimated by Alzheimer's Disease –
the scourge of our rich, so-called developed-
world, he sits alone in a fog of forgetting…
except when lines of Irish poets –
Yeats, Kavanagh, Heaney –
are recited and his face lights up and
the lines finish themselves from his mouth,
from some place most think forgotten.

After that, I went just down the road
to the land of a man of my own age now –
seventy – who has created a sanctuary –
the word is not ill-used – a holy word –
for hurt, lost and rejected cats,
as well as deer, random birds, wild turkeys
and bears, who visit his porch regularly.
I sweep and clean and feed the cats,
all the while listening to this intelligent
large-hearted man, whose softness
compels him to relieve suffering,
his real purpose in the world
though he is a precise and
creative builder.

All this, in one ordinary Friday morning
before noon, shines like bright sun
on March snow.
I have to shade the eyes of my heart
from all the hidden goodness.
I have to allow my heart to expand
and glow with gratitude, breathing it in,
breathing it out.

There is so much more to the world
than I can see. There is so much more
than I can judge or understand,
caught as I so often am
in my categories and limited perceptions
of how things are, or – worse, and smaller –
how they should be. Instead,

the surprising light of what is hidden in the heart
when the mind is too busy analysing, evaluating,
categorizing, deciding –
that is the real treasure, the real joy,
and what sustains life
when all the mind's separations, evaluations,
decisions of what is good and what is bad –
all the mind's follies –
fall to the ground around that small
nearly unnoticeable shaft of light.

So whenever my mind demands – as it so often does –
"do something more important than talking
to someone who won't remember
as soon as you go out the door,"
or "what? Cleaning up after cats and
coaxing them back into trusting people?"
Whenever that voice
makes itself heard as it often often does –

Glimpses

I stop and remember John's eyes, reciting Yeats,
living every word in his confused mind and
crippled body. And I remember Don, lit
with joy as he speaks to his rejected cats,

and I consider myself given heavenly gifts
in the moments I am privileged
to be in their presence.

Presence

This warm, purring cat, nose snuggled
into the crook of my left elbow, demands
that I be here, vibrating with life
as she is now.
Not reading or writing,
or thinking – but present, being here
with what is – Now,
both of us warmly wrapped
in the still silence
just before dawn.

She calls me to it, sending
vibrations through my whole body,
feet burning, body filling
with Presence.
Presence.

It's Enough

It's enough to sit here,
held in the dark silence
of pre-dawn, held in hands
of no more words, no more
writing –
just held in a
moment of pulsing aliveness
needing nothing else.

My heart beats. My breath
rhythmically connects me
to the whole breathing earth.
Things growing
beneath the ground are already
stirring – in a few weeks, they
will show their heads, breaking
ground to see and be seen,
to be welcomed into the Light.

All of it, including me,
emerges from the dark silence
(and eventually returns to it)
of days and years. All of it
moving and flowing through
time. I ride on that never-stopping
flowing current. I surrender
to being taken, no longer
knowing where to step next,
except in the most miniscule
way, lost – the next moment –

in what Time decrees.
It's enough.
Enough.

II.

The time has arrived
for shedding and sharing –
treasures of books and clothes
no longer needed, no longer
treasures for anyone but me.
And that treasure is long past,
a shining star as far away
as the tiny dots of light in the sky
each evening, gone by morning.

A new morning is opening to me,
and the old stars – always
in memory – are treasured
by no one else. Gently,
filling me with streams of Light
(like the Northern Lights now)
they dissolve, but they
will never leave. They are
my shaping, deeper than
the garments I wear,
(though they are that too)
settling me into profound peace.

Enough. My whole adventurous
wonderful life, gift of my Mother
is enough.

Emptying

With my usual books piled
before me in this dark early morning
I can't open one. The books
are closed to me now —
any books. Trying to read
a poem or two of my own
is even a stretch — and
writing in my journal (a usual
daily activity for years
upon years) is
out of the question now.
My hand
will not reach for a pen
nor a journal to write in…

All I can do now
is sit at the table in the
dark and its slow
surrendering to light, allowing
the emptying that is not
initiated by me, but to which
I must surrender. No other
choice is left to me. I am
being taken — in what
I hope is Grace — the grace
of surrender, trust and
opening to a Mystery
of Being I never knew before.

My soul glows. Empty,
It has space to receive.
Tears temper the
arriving flame –

In the Fullness

The fullness of life
lives here in this
hidden forest. All
creatures, including
ourselves, creatures
in the house and outside
of it harmonizing through
season after season,
dark and light,
dawn and twilight
blessed by stars
and moon so vivid
that they seem touchable!

And the silence! The silence
is so thick that it is
like being wrapped
in a protective blanket!

Winds of Soul
SoulWind's embrace!

Home

I thought I was writing poems –
books of them – but now –
reading them years later, I am
stunned to find, reluctantly
(I might admit) – that they
"came through me", that I never
composed them or
thought them through.

And now, now I turn
and receive my own words,
my own given wisdom, needing
it now even more than when
I wrote it down years ago.

Life is a vessel, holding
Space for constant, unending
Transformation. Surrender is
what is asked of me,
Receiving – not searching
now, nor deciding, nor choosing,
but seeing what is
already there, already given,
already waiting, to be received
with open arms
in a long embrace.

Home. Home.

Ashes

When too many ashes gather
inside a woodstove, full burning
is slowed down
almost to no burning at all.

But take out the old ashes,
leaving only those glowing
with light and heat, and
fire leaps alive, wrapping
and dancing with the log
just placed –

And don't the "old ashes"
of everything – memories
especially – prevent life's
full fire – light and
warmth, aliveness glowing –
in our lives too? What
is gone, let be gone.

Celebrate what was
by releasing it into
the Universe.

Spacing the Day

Finally, hours open up as if
long held secrets are finally
offered for revelation, secrets
unable to come forth without
the space given to them
to emerge. These are secrets
not only of the heart, but of the
soul, the deep inner soul
that is the source and shaper
of all life.

So when schedules lose
their power, lightly held and
filled with empty spaces, another
light emerges
in surprising grace, and a pulsing,
previously unknown, pushed
and crowded as it was into hours –
laid out in clock time
and physical places –

now – now there is both
time and space for the heart's
vibrating, quiet sounding
to be felt and heard.

And isn't it the heart that
walks us through every day and night?
Isn't it the heart's rhythm
that determines our being, our
very presence in this time.
this place? And isn't is the
heart with her partner –
the rhythm of breath –
that walks us through
all the other presences that
we take into our eager lives?

And it is up to us, up to me,
to open time's unfolding,
to space the day so that these
deeper, stronger presences
of life's necessity can be recognized
and held with thanks and joy.

Poem of an Ordinary Day

Every day, from waking
in the silent darkness
to early sleep
when she – darkness –
returns again –
every night –
all a poem.

Feeding the cat and dog,
walking into emerging light,
tea before the day begins
deciding the evening meal
feeling the embrace of trees
wrapped in forest silence –
on it goes, a litany of earth's love –
but always, always
the silence.

Just notice. Just notice.

Sitting in the Dark
(for Keith, my long departed brother)

This morning sitting at a table
strewn with books, unable to
open them – it's the book of
my heart that stretches open.

Old memories, vivid experiences, open
like doors into other worlds.
This morning it's my brother
Keith – envious of my invitation
to help wounded animals
at the wildlife center. He
needed no center – he did
this caring alone, in his cabin,
overjoyed when they – weasels,
hawks, owls and others –
could go back to their wild homes,
healed by his attentive caring.

So this morning – decades after
his death - - I feel him near,
urging me to go, as I struggled with
and resisted this invitation, this
privilege, for the past few days,

Keith brings me to yes.

This dark morning silence,
my daily tabernacle,
confirms it, wrapping me
round, as it does each morning,
with a shawl of comfort

sitting in the dark.

For Robert*: Home

When you guided me home
to my own heart, I – full
of wonder – felt I had entered
a whole new world. I had
found Home. Everything –
every leaf, branch,
tiny ground-growth, cloud, star,
flower, grass – need
I go on?

And especially,
especially other people – that
softening opened a knowing
I would never have found
except for your miraculous
and deep discovery of the
presence opened by entering
One's Heart.

So – as you gather all the
amazing discoveries and offerings
of your life, may your own Heart
open even further, even deeper,
so you can know and dwell
in all you have given to
the world – you will never know
the extent of it all, but you
can sense and trust
and hear from those of us
many, many who have received

miracles we would never,
never have known without
your faithfulness to your
own Heart's knowing.

Live into it all, Robert,
and let it take you
Home!

*(Robert Sardello was my longtime teacher of Heart Presence practices for many years. He changed the focus of my life, deepening it, enriching it, grounding it in the whole universe.)

Release

I am dropping into a chasm –
new- unfamiliar -where nothing
is calling me. Some call it
an opening…somewhere in it is
light, but not yet. It is
mine only to wait (finally)
not to make it happen. This
is a strange place, unfamiliar
corners and caves calling –
is it rest they offer? Is it
a kind of completion, or a
new deepening I didn't
know was in me, a gift
long held in disguise?

And do I need to know?

Release, release – be carried,
Be cared for. Open your heart to
the nourishing gifts you are being
offered – only
accept, receive and open –
open your heart to grace and to
gratitude, streaming in the shafts
of light penetrating the darkness.

You are nearly Home.

Loving the Night

Perhaps I love the night
for its silence, it's emptiness
of phone calls and visitors,
expected and unexpected.

And the darkness that thickens
that blanket of silence, deepening
and comforting. I feel the trees
sigh along with me with relief,

echoing and magnifying my own
thankfulness.

Presence

Each morning, now that the woodstove
is no longer the main heat source
in this late spring,
MaCushla climbs into my arms
as soon as I settle at the kitchen table
with my tea and books.
I am now her daily source
of warmth and comfort. She settles
in my arms,
purring herself to sleep.

I am unable to read or write
while she is here. It is
my time of deep and wordless
contemplation, a presence
calling me, teaching me
to be still, to listen,
to be present. Now.

Together we inhabit
the first hour of the day,
watching darkness turn
to Light, alive with
Presence to the unfolding
Moments, whatever –
whatever they may bring.

And whatever the moments of the day
will bring, they are passing thoughts
compared to the Great Stillness,
welcoming, embracing, holding
everything, everything,
with tender welcoming arms, just as
every morning, I hold MaCushla –
Presence.

Doorway* (Thanksgiving Day 2020)

The words of others have lost their meaning
for now – I am sitting here with
my morning tea, empty – not
waiting, just empty. A lovely
way to be on Thanksgiving Day,
having received and received
and received since birth, really –
since wailing into the world. Now
I am full, at least for this moment.
Strange – fullness and emptiness
turning out to be the same
beggar's bowl.

Who am I to know the world?
Who am I to be full in
a swirl of emptiness, neverending?

I only know the doorway, and
have known it for a long time –
perhaps forever –

the open possibility of morning's
dark silence; the unpredictable
blessings and unforeseen losses;
the stunning arrival
of dawn, slow and steady and sure,
opening a day like a cover
taken off a dark well –
and its closing at night, calming
and star-filled, covering everything,

everything, in stillness —
and the Doorway always,
always open.

It is not only in the quiet moments,
the planned opening, the eager receptivity,
the invitation to fill the emptiness:
it is the Emptiness itself. It is
the eternal Unfolding, never stopping,
carrying me onward —
my heart opens, mind waiting
her turn (thanks, but not now)
and fall into
the Empty Nourishing DarkLight.

Lit By Stars/Holding Us All

The yellow tulips
are drinking the water
in their vase, so it seems,
so fast is it going down,
and the flowers opening up.

And MaCushla is occupying
the crook of my left arm
as I write this poem,
snoring loudly, paw between
my breasts, head resting
on my chest. The wall heaters
are blessing the house
with their warm breeze. Windows
are all still dark: no light
yet arriving.

And I notice that the
ordinary noises of everyday life
arrive with dawn's first light,
and leave when that light goes
all those hours later.

Last night I went outside
just before bed and
felt a shoot of exhilaration at
the black sky lit
with shining lights of stars,
and with silence-deep
silence, a blanket of comfort
lit only by stars and a half moon.

And so the world – no-
the universe – renews herself
night after night,
silence after silence, that
comforting blanket
holding us all-
holding us all.

Led By Light

I am led – as surely as a leashed dog,
a bridled horse, or a reined donkey-
I am led by Light – appearing and
shining in the most unexpected places:
thick forest, horizon's clouded edge,
my own mind – and heart.

In the thick of darkness,
inner and outer, day or night,
a stream of Light will suddenly
appear, opening and expanding
my fearful closed heart, and
lifting me – like a small crying child
with arms open and raised to be
taken up into bigger stronger arms
of safety and comfort.

Such is prayer: surrender to the
Great Unknown, whose Light
waits to surprise me in the often
thick darkness of my own heart.

Words

Words have always been the waves
on which my tiny boat rides
both in calm and in wind, whipping
the waves so that all I see are
the walls of the wave itself.

I wait for the calming – I do not –
repeat – do not make it myself,
though through so many years
I am aware that trust in the coming
calm has deepened. Riding the waves-
rather than drowning in the
frustration of expressing them
brings me more quickly to the place
of calm waters, even while a storm
of windy words swirls on and on.

It is the bright but waning moon
that reminds me of this. Shining
brilliantly even as it slowly wanes-
calls me to look – to look through
the kitchen window as she lights
the dawn darkness. And how
does she move so clearly,
intently, without seeming to move
at all? Now there is a naked branch
across her face, where there
was nothing a minute ago!

Glimpses

"This is how you move," she says
to me – "slowly, steadily, still
shining and bright, even while
fading slowly, slowly…
you will know."

And so I do.

And a strange perfume fills the air.

Resting in Light

The mind's release is slow –
more loosening than stopping,
more stretching out –
an elastic band caught before breaking.
Ideas and things-to-do
make lists in my mind, which then
beg to be written – only then
am I released into
the Large and Empty Light
of Soul's waiting. Longer and
longer I sink into it, lists
and must-do's taking
second place for longer
and longer periods of time.

One day, no lists, no obligations
will be left at all. LightSpace
will open her arms, and I will
walk into them, carried and held,
an infant surrendered and
resting – finally – in Light.

The Sea Herself

Time has always been my saviour –
the planning of it, fixed schedules
to count on, to anticipate –
but now, now – Time is a cracking-
open iceberg, dissolving, parts
melting and falling into the
constantly moving sea – I become
the sea herself, shaped by wind
and weather, stillness to be sought
and fought for, precarious
and delicate – yet –

Stillness too arises, even if
its times are brief and unpredictable,
not always at sought times
fitting into planned structures – no –

stillness arises within, not
predictable or controlled or timed,
but like the Sea Herself –

opening and deepening, and –
surprise – comforting in her
still and silent depths –

Stillness. A gift and grace,
patiently waiting for me
when I lay down the pen
and close all the books.

No Words: Morning Comfort

No words will save me now – none
except my own – words that arise
unplanned, even unsought, from
the deepest inner silence
I have ever known.

All my life I have run
from this silence, finding the
words of others to cover
and often express – my own. Now
others' words don't suffice,
can't come near to describing this
daily experience – a full emptiness,
an indescribably Presence,

a knowing beyond describing:
Being. Here. Now.

II

MaCushla, curled up in my arms,
her head leaning into my chest,
holds her ear against my heart.
She is sleeping, sometimes snoring.
Is she hearing my heartbeat?
Is she finding comfort
in its steady, dependable
drumming? Is my heartbeat
her morning comfort as it is mine?

Glimpses

These morning moments, hurrying
through as steadily as the river
not far from our door, are treasures –
never to be lost, but someday,
someday taken, as I step
over that infinite line
into a restful place where
all else will meet in peace
and gratitude and wide smiles
of coming home.

Shimmering

These mornings – still dark –
plunge me into a sense of
my whole life shimmering,
as if I were a raindrop hanging
precariously from a leaf.

One raindrop, carefully observed,
carries a light, even if there is
no sun to reflect it – no sun
but a pale dawn light, calling –
calling it forth into vision, into
being seen, held in the eyes
of someone, anyone, before it drops
to earth, contributing her
small moisture to thirsty ground.

And so do I – though my tiny drop
is getting smaller – except – except –
when words such as these arrive unbidden
and I write them down!
Words from Heart,
not from Mind,
which is the necessary channel
but not their source.

Only Heart can offer the Shimmering,
Only Heart.

Arriving

The softness of the air
is the pillow of its silence –
noises – ordinary – footsteps,
dog barks, do not disturb
the silence. It receives them,
holds them tenderly, like
innocent children. Spring
is arriving – here – opening
and holding everything in
tender arms, whispering
to the softening earth – "it's time,
it's time" nudging the green to
come forth, to show her fresh
emergence coming alive,
coming alive, bringing
and ringing in Spring!

Rest

"I am wandering
in the dense forest
of my past life, marvelling
at the shoots of wisdom
that shoot up like unsought
flowers, and then allowed
to fade and disappear
as flowers do. I cannot
cling to them, but they save
my life in the moments when
they appear, before I am
claimed again by worry and
hurry, my two worse friends.
Still, I know now that the
moments will come, will
come, when light will open
my inner heart and I will
rest. Rest.

Finally

I used to think that coming home
To myself was a way to speak about
Refocusing my mind, my heart, my very
Spirit. Now - finally - at this late time
in my life-threatening I finally realize
That coming home to myself is also
(And perhaps foundationally)
Coming home to my body -
Finally finally inhabiting at 75-
Shyly, with resistance (don't I have
Better things to do?) Taking time
to breathe slowly and deeply;
Stopping intentionally, paying
Attention to the moment, and not
Only the hour or the day....oh the
shifts-- Many and often too many.

Then I am a child, petulant and resistant
Or deeply happy and lit with inner joy.
Neither of them lasts - nothing lasts -
But I ride the waves of whatever is
And relinquish seeing ahead of time
What I hope for or fear. Whatever
Is, just whatever is in that moment-
is my doorway to eternal light.

Womb of the World

The only think that calls me now
is silence. I have tried the news,
stories of many kinds,
detectives – even weather
predictions – but they are empty
sounds on a hollow drum.
Silence – only Silence –
is full, and full of
life for me. It is Silence that
is calling – a soft loud voice
with open arms – into which
I run for comfort and holding,
for support and safety. Silence.

Silence is the womb of the world.

Deep Surrender: Gutted

All my life, even as a child, I
rode time in a little boat on waves
too high to see past –
with welcome calm between the
pushing and heaving, between
the rowing and resting –
it was all – all predictable
and so – comforting.

Now there is no predicting,
no soothing schedule –
each day opens windows on
the unexpected, offers unplanned
gifts and surprising
(not so welcome)
Challenges. All grace. All
Grace.
Now is the time for choosing
deep surrender to a world grown
bigger, deeper, more in turmoil,
in wars – dissolving structures and
daily surprises – than I could
ever, ever have imagined, attached
as I was and still clinging
to a predictable world
now dissolving – every second
dissolving before us.

Such is the nature of Now.
Such is the invitation into
larger Life. Such are the slowly
appearing arms of death, of the known
and always present stream of light
signaling the Unknown,
its arms offering comfort –
and inviting surrender.

Gutted, as our old fishermen would say –
totally gutted – is what
deep surrender brings about.
The unclaimed insists on being claimed!

Only in Silence, Only in Light

The fullness of Life is this:
sitting in the early morning silence,
full of Presence, full with possibility,
watching Dawn Light claim
the world. Oh yes – I know how
it all happens, but in seventy – six
years I have not come to
understand (and never will) the
miraculous majesty of it, the
dependability of it, the silent
presence of it, giving not only
Light to the world, but nourishment,
and the grace to be found
(actually, received) only – only
in Silence, only in Light.

And I – a tiny negligible creature –
leaving the world sooner rather than
later – glowing with awe, overflowing
with daily grace ---
arms out to Mystery.

Empty Fullness: Cosmos of the Heart

I sit here listening to the silence,
a warm summer day, cat and
dog my quiet companions –
but it's the silence, thick
with empty fullness, no sound
really – no sound – though
the outdoor chimes make their
voices heard, even without
the wind. But it is the Silence,
the Earth's own voice, that
is speaking today in its thick
presence. Comforting, holding –
not just me, but everything
and everyone. No blade of grass
or tiny insect is too small or of
little value – the Silence values
holds and carried everything,
every miniscule presence
of existence, I being one of them.

The Empty Fullness of Silence
is the world, a Cosmos of the Heart.

Home

Another layer now rises from the
endless inner depths: I see – I see
more fully for the first time –
how my life has unfolded and unfolded
and unfolded. It was always saved by
achievement, by doing what was
expected and approved by anyone
who mattered – all imprints of my Mother
who made fear my inner roots of growth
from earliest age, before I was even
a year old. Thus, my lifetime of
conforming, pleasing, helping, saving.

It was really myself I was saving,
Always myself. And I did –
Save myself – until now, at
Seventy-six, I walk into
A Light never seen before,
Never even suspected. A Light
waiting to bring me Home.

The Great Emptiness*

The Great Emptiness has opened —
finally I name it — and it is
claiming all of me. Nothing
feels familiar, ordinary, even
safe — a strange unfamiliarity,
a momentary forgetting of ordinary
daily things, an inner distancing —
these are my daily, ordinary
experiences now. No small detail
is automatic — I focus to recall
and eventually it arises, but automatic
remembering is no longer
to be counted on —

I read all the poems I have
published over the past decades,
and the ones I am still writing
now — astounded, truly shocked
at the wisdom that has poured —
literally poured out from my heart
these many many years!

Gifts — all of them — not
from me, but through me.

So now – now it's time (finally
I am able to not only admit
but comprehend) to receive,
receive – and open
every fibre of my being
so that the stream of Light,
that Universal Light, can pass
through me into the world!

This morning's dream as I awoke: I am a dark shadow outline, standing in front of a large window, looking out on an all-white landscape. No trees, nor any form is visible. I am framed by a large picture widow, and a kind of dawn, a just awakening light, is all I can see on the horizon. And perhaps the reason I have not been able to meditate for so long is just this avoidance – the Emptiness – nothing else will come – old and many methods and ways to meditate hold no foundation or framework for me any longer. There is only the emptiness, and looking into it the only reality – perhaps, perhaps I am again alone in the little boat, tossed on a stormy seas, surrender my only choice. And now MaCushla has come to comfort me, lying in my arms for nearly an hour, purring and napping -this warm budly in my arms, one hand free to write…

It is I who must surrender to this emptiness, to this sense of my own life gone, and to grieve, to grieve, even while opening to whatever is calling me that I cannot yet hear. There is only the emptiness…and the knowing… and the naming, only in and through that emptiness…(June 7, 2023)

Eggshells

I write these words in pencil*, so
meager and transparent and delicate
a day seems, plans like eggshells
scattered on the ground – to be
walked on without thought,
without clinging or attachment.

The world – shivering with
pandemic fear – and now –
of this thick smoke from wild fires
both East and West – has become
a place of
desperation
turmoil
denial
and
despair –
everything as changeable
as erasing these
pencilled words.

There is no going back. And the
summer weather this year is an
exclamation mark to it all, with its
extreme heat dropping to cold
and back again in a matter
of a day.

Light Arrives

Even when rain pounds the roof
or snow obscures vision,
dawn still arrives, bringing light
to whatever world
is showing itself
in early morning –
light arrives,
giving darkness its
time to sleep,
to wrap another part
of this tender, struggling planet
in
restoring arms.

Silence:
(moments of emptiful)

I sit within the fullness of Day
before Light has even fully arrived.
It is heralded by Silence.
It is held in Silence.
It is the Presence of Silence –
thick and still,
holding everything, everything –
within its
unfathomable
welcoming
arms.

Beside the Point

All the words of all the years
Have led me here, brought
Me here, truth be told,
But now
They fall into unseen depths
Like stones thrown by a child
From a solid shore.

Sitting in the early morning silence
thick with Presence,
I know myself
held and carried like a newborn,
able to feel…present
but only that.
only that.

Doing anything else feels
beside the point.

Fallen Away

So it has come to this:
there is only the Silence.
Its thick presence is not
disturbed by chirping birds –
the Silence holds them as
it does me. Words and writing –
even poems – stand waiting,
but unable to enter the
Presence of Silence.

I am held in the most
Profound Peace. But only –
only – when I am empty
of all else that has filled
my life as if I were
a shopping cart. Empty now,
Silence fills me, wraps me round
Like an infant blanket.

All Else Falls Away
Loretta Dower, RSM: a tribute

The air is thick with waiting.
Nothing else is possible.
I am wrapped in it
like a blanket, waiting –
for the phone to ring
to tell me –
She's gone.
She's gone…

All while knowing
that she will never be gone.
That I was formed and live
my life (have always lived it)
from her generous shaping, from
her encouragement and trust,
from her love – brave,
affirming, and daring me
to be myself, to offer
all my gifts to the community
and to the larger world.

She sent me out, pushing me
to follow what drew me, never
withdrawing her encouragement.
Affirmation, and love.

Living her own struggles
as she crossed the roiling river
from the old ways in which
she was shaped and formed –

to the new: ways of change,
of opening, of a freedom
never before known – and
hesitantly lived – Loretta
struggled often, and also braved
her way into the unknown,
into times we now take for granted.
Her hesitant anxiety masked
her deep vision, her
loving connections,
her soulful engagement
with an emerging world, until…
until she could step no further,
and knew she had reached
the end that we all reach –
that unknown moment of
stepping over
the hidden limit, waiting
to lead us
into the next world.
She has
taken that step. She is
looking around in wonder.
And she waits for us all,
For Loretta might leave this life,
but she will never leave the hearts
of those she loved,
of those she served,
and who loved her, year after year,
deepening into Light.

Eternal Light has
claimed Loretta now.
And she is at peace – the peace
that awaits us all, the peace
that makes possible the next step.

May she rest in eternal peace.
May she deepen the peace that
the rest of us are seeking.

And may she greet us with peace
when the moments of our own
slipping out and stepping over
arrives.

(Brenda Peddigrew, RSM/ July 4, 2023)

www.ingramcontent.com/pod-product-compliance
Lightning Source LLC
LaVergne TN
LVHW091549060526
838200LV00036B/758